Contents

Chapter 1   Buying a lottery ticket   6
Chapter 2   She's leaving home   10
Chapter 3   Winning the lottery   14
Chapter 4   The taxi   18
Chapter 5   Trains to Glasgow?   20
Chapter 6   Rick stops a taxi   22
Chapter 7   Goodbye, lottery ticket   26
Chapter 8   Where am I? Who am I?   29
Chapter 9   It's like winning the lottery!   32

People in the story

 **Rick** plays the guitar and writes songs

 **Mary** is Rick's wife

 **Barry Green** is running from the police

 **Sarah** is a singer

Cambridge English Readers

Starter Level

Series . Philip Prowse

What a Lottery!

Colin Campbell

CAMBRIDGE

CAMBRIDGE UNIVERSITY PRESS

Cambridge, New York, Melbourne, Madrid, Cape Town, Singapore, São Paulo, Delhi

Cambridge University Press
The Edinburgh Building, Cambridge CB2 8RU, UK

www.cambridge.org
Information on this title: www.cambridge.org/9780521683272

First published 2006
3rd printing 2008

Colin Campbell has asserted his right to be identified as the Author of the Work in
accordance with the Copyright, Design and Patents Act 1988.

Printed in the United Kingdom at the University Press, Cambridge

Illustrations by Hannah Webb

A catalogue record for this publication is available from the British Library

ISBN 978-0-521-68327-2 paperback
ISBN 978-0-521-68328-9 paperback plus audio CD pack

Places in the story

Chapter 1 *Buying a lottery ticket*

Rick Drummond is going to buy a lottery ticket. He's walking down the street and listening to music. The music is very loud. Rick is singing as he listens. He walks into an ice-cream shop.

'Can I help you?' the shop assistant asks Rick. Rick looks at the man, but he can't hear him.

'Sorry?' Rick says.

The shop assistant writes something and gives it to Rick. It says: TURN YOUR MUSIC OFF!

'Sorry,' Rick says. He turns off his music. 'Can I have a lottery ticket, please?'

The shop assistant smiles. 'This is an ice-cream shop,' he says. 'We don't sell lottery tickets.'

'But I always buy my lottery ticket here, from Mr Khan. Where is he?' says Rick.

'Mr Khan's shop is next door and he sells lottery tickets,' the shop assistant says slowly.

'Ah, I've got the wrong shop. Stupid me!' says Rick.

'Well,' asks the shop assistant, 'do you want to buy an ice-cream?'

'No, thank you,' says Rick. 'Ice-cream is bad for me. See you.'

'Why? What do you do?' the shop assistant asks.

Rick turns and smiles at the man. 'I play the guitar and I write songs. I'm going to be a famous rock star one day.'

Rick leaves the shop. He's singing a new song.

'It's an ice-cream shop, baby,
You can't buy a lottery ticket here,
It's an ice-cream shop, baby,
No lottery tickets here.'

The shop assistant watches him. 'He can't sing and he writes stupid songs. He isn't going to be a rock star!' He laughs.

Chapter 2 *She's leaving home*

Rick buys a lottery ticket from Mr Khan and goes back to his house. He's trying to think of the next words for his ice-cream song.

'Hey, Mary, I'm home! Are you here?' he shouts.

'No, I'm in China,' Mary answers from the bedroom. Rick doesn't hear her. He's looking for his guitar. Rick smiles when he sees it. He loves his guitar.

'I've got a new song, Mary. Do you want to hear it?' he asks.

'No!' Mary says.

Rick walks into the bedroom. He doesn't see the very big suitcase in the middle of the room.

Mary closes the suitcase. Then Rick sees it for the first time.

'Hey, Mary, where are we going? Are we going on holiday? Cool!' Rick says.

Mary looks at him sadly.

'No, we're *not* going on holiday,' she says. '*We* are not going anywhere. I'm going to my sister's in Glasgow. *You* are not going anywhere. I'm leaving you.'

'Leaving? When?' Rick asks.

'When? Why don't you ask me why?' Mary says.

'OK then. Why?' Rick asks.

'I can't live with you, Rick. You're going nowhere.' Mary looks at a photo of Rick by the bed. 'You see this?' she asks. 'This photo is ten years old. Look at you. The same Rick – no changes.

'You write your stupid songs and buy your lottery tickets and wait. What are you waiting for? Do something!'

Rick is looking at his guitar and thinking.

'Are you listening to me?' Mary asks him.

'What are you waiting for? That's a good name for a song.' He gets his guitar and starts to play.

'Rick!' Mary takes her suitcase and walks to the front door. She turns and looks at Rick. 'I've got a song for you.' She sings, '*I'm* leaving home, goodbye.'

'That's a Beatles song, isn't it?' Rick asks.

Mary opens the door and leaves.

Chapter 3 *Winning the lottery*

It's Saturday evening, twenty-four hours later, and Rick is still sitting in his flat. His guitar is on the floor and his head is in his hands. The television is on, but Rick isn't watching it. He's thinking about Mary. 'What am I going to do?'

He takes his guitar and starts to play, but then stops again.

Rick looks at the television. 'Number sixteen. Number twenty-three.' It's the lottery. Rick says the numbers after the man. 'Sixteen, twenty-three. I've got those numbers.'

Rick looks for his lottery ticket.

'Number forty-one. Number six. Number nineteen. Number forty-nine. And here are the numbers again.'

Rick finds his ticket. He looks at the numbers on his ticket and at the numbers on the television. He's got all the numbers!

'And the winner tonight gets eight million pounds!'

'Mary! Mary!' Rick says. 'Come here. Quick!' He forgets she isn't there. For a minute he's sad. Then he thinks, 'I'm rich. *We're* rich. I can buy anything. I can play my music and I can be famous. And Mary can … Mary's going to be happy.'

He looks at the ticket again and laughs. Then he sits down. There's a loud noise – he's sitting on his guitar.

'Oh no! My guitar! My beautiful guitar! I …' Then he thinks of the money. 'I can buy lots of guitars now. I must tell Mary.'

He goes to the phone to call her. Then he stops and thinks, 'I can't tell her on the phone! That's not right. But how am I going to tell her?'

He sits down, on the guitar again. There's the same loud noise. Rick doesn't hear it. 'I know. I can write her a new song now. I can go to Glasgow and sing it outside her window. Now that's cool!'

Chapter 4   *The taxi*

It's late and it's dark. Barry Green is walking down the street. The police are looking for him. He must get away quickly. Then a taxi comes down the street. But Barry hasn't got any money and he can't take a taxi. The taxi stops at a petrol station and the driver puts petrol into the taxi. Then he goes into the shop. Barry walks across the street and looks in the taxi.

The keys are still in the car and the taxi driver is still in the shop.

'It's my lucky day,' Barry thinks. He gets into the taxi and drives away.

Chapter 5 *Trains to Glasgow?*

It's ten o'clock. Rick is still in his flat. He's very happy. He has a new song and he's going to see Mary. Everything is going to be OK.

'Wait,' he thinks. 'How am I going to get to Glasgow?' He picks up the phone.

'Hello,' Rick says. 'When is the next train to Glasgow?'

'From where?' a woman asks.

'From here,' Rick says.

'Where's here?' the woman asks again.

'From Wallingford,' Rick answers.

Rick hears the woman on a computer.

'Do you live in Wallingford, sir?' she asks.

'Yes. Why do you ask?' Rick answers.

'There's no train station in Wallingford,' she says.

'Oh yeah, you're right. What about planes?' asks Rick.

There's no answer.

Chapter 6 *Rick stops a taxi*

It's midnight. Rick wants to go to Glasgow but doesn't know how to get there. It's late and there are no trains or buses. He leaves his flat. Then he sees a taxi.

'Taxi! Stop!' Rick runs in front of the taxi and it stops. The driver is Barry Green and he looks very angry.

'What do you want?' Barry asks.

'I'm going to Glasgow,' Rick says.

'Lucky you! Have a nice time. Goodbye,' Barry answers.

'No, you don't understand. I want you to take me. This is a taxi, isn't it?' Rick doesn't take taxis very often. Then he smiles. 'Look,' he says, 'it says "Taxi".'

'I know it's a taxi,' says Barry, 'but I'm not working tonight.' Then Barry thinks, 'I haven't got any money.'

'OK,' he says, 'I can take you to Glasgow, but it's going to be a lot of money. It's five hundred kilometres to Glasgow. That's going to be five hundred pounds.'

Rick smiles. 'Five hundred, five thousand,' he says. 'That's nothing. I've got the winning lottery ticket.' Rick has the ticket in his hand. 'I'm going to get eight million pounds for this ticket!' Rick gets into the taxi.

Barry looks at the ticket in Rick's hand. He looks at the date. It's today's date. He looks at the numbers and then he looks at Rick's face.

'I don't see a name on the ticket,' Barry says.

Rick laughs. 'There aren't any names on lottery tickets.'

'How do they know it's your lottery ticket then?' Barry asks.

Rick laughs again. 'You don't know much about lotteries, do you?' he says. 'I've got the ticket – it's my money. Easy.'

Barry smiles. 'Eight million? You're a lucky man,' he says.

Chapter 7   *Goodbye, lottery ticket*

'I'm never going to work again,' Rick tells Barry.

'Do you work now?' Barry asks.

'No, I don't,' Rick says. 'I play music and write songs. And that's what I'm going to do, all day, every day. And I'm going to buy my wife a ...' Rick stops and thinks. 'I'm going to buy my wife a ... That's funny. I don't know what she wants.'

Barry isn't listening. He's thinking about the eight million pounds.

Barry turns to Rick. 'We're coming to a café. Do you want a coffee?' he asks.

'No, thanks,' Rick answers. 'I only drink tea.'

'Good.' Barry smiles. 'We can have tea.'

They stop and go into the café. 'Sit down,' Barry says, 'and give me some money. I can get the drinks.'

'Am I buying your tea too?' Rick asks.

'You're rich, remember?' Barry says.

Rick gives Barry the money and Barry goes to buy the drinks. Rick sits at the table and takes out the lottery ticket.

Barry comes back with the tea. He sees the ticket in Rick's hand and smiles.

Barry puts the tea down fast on the table. The hot tea goes on to the table, and on to Rick, and on to the ticket.

'Ow!' shouts Rick. 'It's hot. And it's all over the ticket.'

'Give the ticket to me!' shouts Barry and tries to take the ticket. But it's wet with tea. Now Rick has half the ticket and Barry has half.

'Give me your half of the ticket!' Barry shouts.

'The ticket is no good now,' Rick answers. 'There's tea on it and you can't read the numbers. And there are two halves. Goodbye, lottery ticket. Goodbye, eight million pounds.'

'What!' Barry shouts. Then he hears a noise and his face goes white. There's a police car outside the café. Barry turns and runs to the door. Rick gets up and runs after him.

'Stop!' Rick shouts, but he forgets about the tea. Crash! Rick falls and his head hits the table.

Chapter 8   *Where am I? Who am I?*

'Where am I?' asks Rick. He looks at the young woman and asks, 'Am I dead?'

'No, you're in a café.'

'And who are you?'

'I'm Sarah. Who are you? What are you doing on the floor?'

'I'm …' Rick thinks for a minute. He can't remember his name. He can't remember anything. 'I can't remember my name. I can't remember anything,' he says.

'Look in your pockets,' Sarah says. 'Maybe you've got something with your name on it.'

Rick looks. 'No, there's nothing. Wait a minute …' He takes something from his coat pocket and gives it to the girl.

It's a photo of Rick playing his guitar.

'You play the guitar?' Sarah says. 'Can you play this?' she asks. She gives him a guitar.

Rick takes the guitar and starts to play. Very well.

'Wow, you're good!' Sarah says. 'You're very good.'

Rick smiles and starts to sing too. 'Stop! Stop!' Sarah shouts. 'You play very well, but I'm the singer.'

'Sorry?' Rick asks.

'I'm a singer and I'm going to sing tomorrow. But my guitar player isn't coming. He's leaving me. Do you want to come and play with me?'

Rick thinks for a minute. 'Well, I don't know my name, I don't know who I am or where I'm going, so why not? Where are you singing?'

'In Glasgow,' says Sarah.

'Glasgow?' says Rick. He thinks for a minute.

'Are you from Glasgow?' Sarah asks.

'I don't know,' Rick answers.

Chapter 9 *It's like winning the lottery!*

Rick and his new friend walk out of the café. They look very happy. Sarah turns and smiles.

'Aren't I lucky?' she says. 'My guitar player leaves me and I find you in a café!'

A police car drives by. Rick and Sarah don't see Barry in the back of the car.

'Yes,' says Rick. 'I'm lucky too. It's like winning the lottery!'

*   *   *

Sarah and Rick play in Glasgow. Everyone loves them.

'They love us!' Sarah shouts to Rick. 'And who's that woman there? Is she a friend?'

'No,' Rick answers. 'I don't know her.'